INFANTILE

OF

SEXUAL II

# INFANTILE ORIGINS
# OF
# SEXUAL IDENTITY

Herman Roiphe, M.D.,
and
Eleanor Galenson, M.D.

INTERNATIONAL UNIVERSITIES PRESS, INC.

Library of Congress Cataloging in Publication Data
Roiphe, Herman, 1924–
    Infantile origins of sexual identity.

        Bibliography: p.
        Includes index.
        1. Infant psychology. 2. Identity (Psychology)
3. Sex (Psychology) 4. Parent and child.
5. Psychoanalysis. I. Galenson, Eleanor, 1916–
II. Title. (DNLM: 1. Identification (psychology) –
In infancy and childhood. 2. Sex behavior – In
infancy and childhood. WS 105.5.Sr R74li]
BF720.S48R64     155.4'22     81-14290
ISBN 0-8236-2368-8           AACR2